VEGAN
RECIPES FROM THE
MIDDLE EAST

PARVIN RAZAVI

GRUB STREET | LONDON

CONTENTS

FOREWORD

―◇◇◇―

For me, cooking and eating are important social activities because they cut across boundaries, connect people to one another and are a lot of fun! I am delighted to be able to share my joy of cooking with you. The recipes I have created are often very simple, many can be prepared in under half an hour, leaving lots of time to enjoy them!

Being responsible stewards of our resources and using ecological and organic ingredients are very important to me. I particularly value the fact that in each of my creations, the individual components can be tasted and that the ingredients are cooked gently, so that our daily food provides us with energy and does not stress our bodies. In terms of soya products, I have used only soya yogurt for various dips, which can be replaced by any other vegetable-based yogurt, if preferred.

Middle Eastern cuisine is fresh and varied. Apart from the well-known classics, it also offers a whole range of tasty surprises. It is not unusual for up to 10 dishes to be prepared for one meal, known in the Middle East as mezze. Classic courses such as starters and main courses do not exist; it is more common for everything to be served together. In following this principle, I found it natural to embrace various Middle Eastern eating cultures and to combine them with contemporary approaches. This is what I love about cooking: inviting guests to sit down at a large table to experience the diversity of different cultures.

Yours, *Parvin*

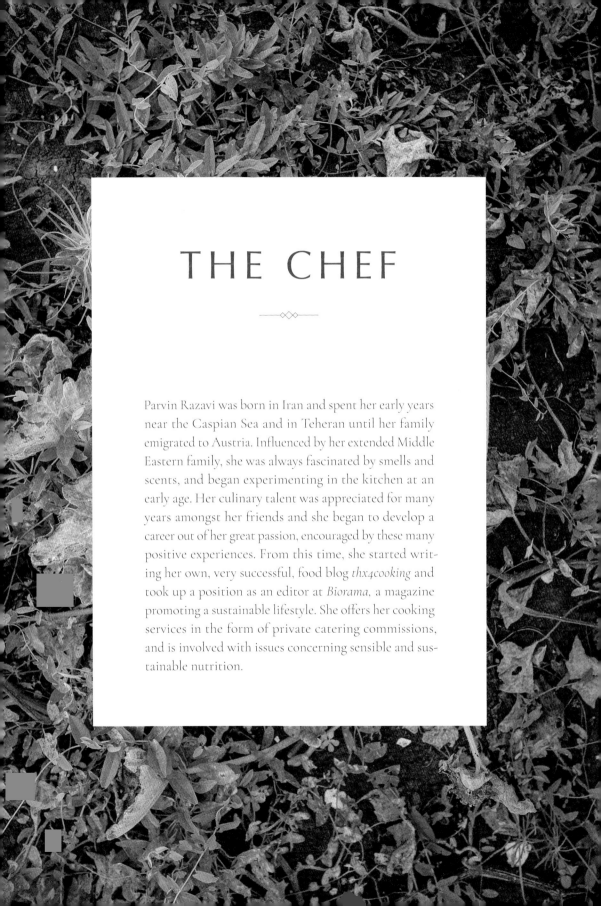

THE CHEF

◇◇

Parvin Razavi was born in Iran and spent her early years near the Caspian Sea and in Teheran until her family emigrated to Austria. Influenced by her extended Middle Eastern family, she was always fascinated by smells and scents, and began experimenting in the kitchen at an early age. Her culinary talent was appreciated for many years amongst her friends and she began to develop a career out of her great passion, encouraged by these many positive experiences. From this time, she started writing her own, very successful, food blog *thx4cooking* and took up a position as an editor at *Biorama*, a magazine promoting a sustainable lifestyle. She offers her cooking services in the form of private catering commissions, and is involved with issues concerning sensible and sustainable nutrition.

GLOSSARY

ALLSPICE - PIMENTO - MYRTLE PEPPER
Bot.: *Pimenta officinalis*
Fam.: *Myrtaceae*
Arabic: *Bhar hub wa na'im, bahar*
Farsi: *Fel fel shirin*
Turkish: *Yeni bahar*

Although pimento is a spice from the New World, it was adopted by the cuisine of the Middle East on account of its compatibility with cloves, cinnamon and nutmeg.

BARBERRIES
Bot.: *Berberis*
Fam.: *Berberidaceae*
Arabic: *barbaris*
Farsi: *zereshk*
Turkish: *kardin tuzlugu*

The berries are dried and are used in Persian cuisine to enhance dishes. They have a fruity, slightly tart taste.

BAY - BAY LEAF
Bot.: *Laurus nobilis*
Fam.: *Lauraceae*
Arabic: *warak al gar*
Greek: *thaphne*
Farsi: *barg-e-bo*
Turkish: *dafne yapregi*

Bay leaves are used in Greek, Turkish and Cypriot cuisines to season stews and marinades.

BLACK-EYED BEANS
Bot.: *Vigna unguiculata*
Fam.: *Leguminosae*
Arabic: *lubyi msallat*
Greek: *fassoulia mavromatica*

Black-eyed beans come from the cowpea family and are originally from central Africa. Black-eyed beans have a pleasant, slightly sweet taste and cook more quickly than other dried beans.

BROAD BEANS

Bot.: *Vicia faba*
Fam.: *Leguminosae*
Arabic: *ful nabed*
Farsi: *baghali*
Greek: *koukia*
Turkish: *fava*

Used fresh in Greek, Cypriot, Turkish and Arabic cuisine. Young beans are often cooked whole in their pods, however ripe beans are cooked after shelling. In Iranian cuisine, the skin of the beans is removed. Frozen broad beans are available year-round in Iranian shops.

BULGUR

Arabic: *burghul, bulkar*
Greek: *pourgouri*
Turkish: *bulgar*

Husked wheat, steamed and toasted, then dried and milled. Bulgur is available in fine and coarse varieties, has a slightly nutty taste and is very popular in Middle Eastern cuisine. Widely available in supermarkets.

CARDAMOM

Bot.: *Ellettaria cardamonum*
Fam.: *Zingiberceae*
Arabic: *hell, hail*
Farsi: *hell*
Greek: *Kardamo*
Turkish: *Kakule tohamu*

An important spice in the Gulf States and in Persian cuisine. Available as pods, seeds or ground. If ground cardamom is called for, it is often better to grind fresh pods with a mortar and pestle. Cardamom is an essential ingredient in Arabic coffee.

CHICKPEAS - GARBANZO BEANS

Bot.: *Cicer arietinium*
Fam.: *Fabaceae*
Arabic: *hummus*
Armenian: *siser-noghud*
Greek: *revithia*
Farsi: *nokhod*
Turkish: *nohut*

Very well-known and used by the ancient peoples of Persia, Egypt and Greece. They are popular throughout the entire region. Should be soaked for at least 12 hours before cooking, but are also available ready-cooked in supermarkets.

CINNAMON

Bot.: *Cinnamomum zeylanicum*
Fam.: *Lauraceae*
Arabic: *darseen, kerfee*
Armenian: *dartchin*
Farsi: *darchin*
Turkish: *tarcin*

A very popular spice. It is used in Middle Eastern cuisine both in spicy and sweet dishes.

Note: It is not necessary to take as much care in terms of quantities when using whole sticks as when using ground cinnamon.

CLOVES
Bot.: *Syzygium aromaticum*
Fam.: *Myrtaceae*
Arabic: *habahan, gharanful-mesmar*
Farsi: *nebos*
The dried flower buds of the evergreen clove tree are a very popular spice in Middle Eastern cuisine.

CORIANDER
Bot.: *Coriandrum sativum*
Fam.: *Umbelliferae*
Arabic: *kazbarah*
Farsi: *geshniez*
Turkish: *kisniz*
From the parsley family. The leaves and the seeds are used in Middle Eastern cookery. It is hard to imagine Persian cuisine without coriander leaves and it is always served fresh at every meal in conjunction with various other herbs.

CUMIN
Bot.: *Cuminum cyminum*
Fam.: *Umbelliferae*
Arabic: *kamoon*
Farsi: *zire*
Turkish: *cemen*
Cumin plays an important role in North African and Middle Eastern cookery. Its full flavour develops on heating. Cumin is one of my absolute favourite spices and I could not imagine my kitchen without it.

DILL
Bot.: *Anethum graveolens*
Fam.: *Umbelliferae*
Arabic: *shabath*
Armenian: *samit*
Farsi: *shewid*
Turkish: *dereotu*
Dill originally comes from the Mediterranean area and has a fresh, bitter aroma. It goes excellently with vegetables, rice and pickles.

FAVA BEAN - FIELD BEAN - ENGLISH BEAN
Bot.: *Vicia faba*
Fam.: *Fabaceae*
Arabic: *Foul*
Turkish: *Bakla*
Also known as Windsor bean, pigeon bean and horse bean. Is only used in its dried form. They range in colour from beige to purple. The beans must be soaked for at least 12 hours and be cooked very slowly. A good alternative is precooked broad beans in tins or jars.

FENNEL SEEDS
Bot.: *Foeniculum vulgare*
Fam.: *Umbelliferae*
Arabic: *shamaar*
Farsi: *rayianeh*
Greek: *finokio*
Turkish: *reyene*

A fine spice with an aniseed-like aroma that can be used instead of dill. Goes well with vegetables, particularly fennel, and gives every dish a delicate aroma.

FENUGREEK
Bot.: *Trigonella foenum-graecum*
Fam.: *Leguminosae*
Arabic: *hulba, hilbeh*
Farsi: *shambelileh*
Greek: *trigonella, moschositaro*
Turkish: *cemen, poy baharati*
The fresh leaves are used in many Persian dishes and are available as dried herbs in Iranian shops.

GARLIC
Bot.: *Allium sativum*
Fam.: *Liliaceae*
Arabic: *tum*
Greek: *skortho*
Farsi: *sir*
Turkish: *sarmisak*
Garlic has a healing effect on the body and is an essential ingredient in the cuisines of the Middle East and the Mediterranean. Care should be taken when frying it: burnt garlic tastes bitter. In Iran, whole bulbs of garlic are pickled in vinegar which preserves them for up to 20 years. Medicinal properties are attributed to this pickled garlic. Garlic is also used to decorate the traditional festive table known as the "haft-seen", the "seven gifts" at Nowruz, Persian New Year, celebrated around 21 March in Iran, Afghanistan, Tajikistan and Central Asia.

LIME, DRIED

Arabic: *loomi, noomi, noomi besra*
Farsi: *limoo amani*
Dried limes are also called black limes and are available in almost all the Gulf States. In Persian cuisine, dried limes are used in many different types of stew. Originally, this greeny-yellow citrus fruit came from Oman and was left to dry on the tree itself. Dried limes are available from Iranian shops. If you have a food dehydrator, you can dry them yourself. They produce a refreshing aroma when grated over vegetables or salads.

MINT

Bot.: *Mentha spicata or Mentha viridis*
Fam.: *Labiatae*
Arabic: *na'na*
Farsi: *nana*
Turkish: *nane*
The most popular mint in the Middle East is spearmint. It is very popular and frequently used, both fresh and dried. Mint

gives every Middle Eastern dish an inviting and enticing flavour. Dried mint helps to prevent flatulence when eating legumes, and it is liberally sprinkled over dishes in Persian cuisine. Dried mint is heated with oil and added to dishes that include legumes.

OKRA - LADY'S FINGERS

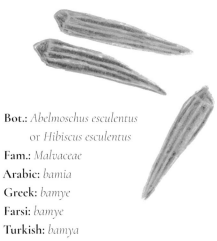

Bot.: *Abelmoschus esculentus* or *Hibiscus esculentus*
Fam.: *Malvaceae*
Arabic: *bamia*
Greek: *bamye*
Farsi: *bamye*
Turkish: *bamya*

Okra has an angular pod in the shape of a cone. Its sticky and slimy consistency is not always popular. There are methods for removing the mucilage, which involve putting the okra in diluted vinegar before using. Young okra pods are popular because they are less sticky.

PINE NUTS

Bot.: *Pinus pinea*
Fam.: *Pinaceae*
Arabic: *snoober*
Greek: *koukounaria*
Farsi: *chehel o ghooze*
Turkish: *cam sistigi*

Are used in many recipes hailing from the Middle East, the Mediterranean and North Africa. Pine nuts enhance any recipe when roasted or cooked in dishes due to their mild, sweet and unobtrusive flavour. They contain a number of mono- and polyunsaturated fatty acids. Pine nuts are also rich in protein, carbohydrates, minerals and trace elements.

PISTACHIOS

Bot.: *Pistacia vera*
Fam.: *Anacardiaceae*
Farsi: *pesteh*

Pistachios are some of the oldest flowering cultivated plants and are indigenous to the Middle East. Both savoury and sweet, they are a staple part of eastern, and now, western cuisine. My favourite pistachios come from Iran.

POMEGRANATE

Bot.: *Punica granatum*
Fam.: *Punicaceae*
Arabic: *Roumman*
Farsi: *anar*
Greek: *rodi*
Turkish: *nar*

A historical fruit and valued by the ancient Persians as the fruit of paradise for its healing properties. Pomegranates can be stored for months in a cool, dry place. The juice or syrup is an essential ingredient in Persian and Iranian cuisine and is very popular on account of its sweet and sour aroma. The syrup and the seeds are also cooked in recipes or used to garnish dishes in countries such as Lebanon and Syria.

RAS EL HANOUT

A Moroccan spice mix of muscat, coriander, cinnamon, kukuma, cumin, ginger and clove. Depending on the type of production, the spice mixture is composed rather sweetly, sharply or more bitterly.

ROSEWATER

Arabic: *Ma'el ward*
Farsi: *Golab*
Turkish: *Gül suyu*

Rosewater is an essential water derived from the rose or *Rosa centifolia*, which occurs as a by-product when distilling rose oil from rose petals. It is used for both spicy and sweet dishes. Because there are differences in quality, each new brand should be tested for its intensity and then used appropriately.

SAFFRON

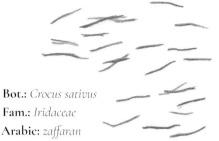

Bot.: *Crocus sativus*
Fam.: *Iridaceae*
Arabic: *zaffaran*
Farsi: *za'faran*

The stigmas of almost a quarter of a million saffron flowers are needed to produce 500 grams of saffron. It is therefore hardly surprising that saffron has been long one of the most expensive spices in the world. Saffron is ground in a pestle with a sugar cube, then dissolved and steeped in hot water before being used. This helps it to develop its special flavour and remarkable colour.

SESAME

Bot.: *Sesamum indicum*
    or *Sesamum orientale*
Fam.: *Pedaliaceae*
Arabic: *simsum*
Greek: *sousame*
Farsi: *konjet*
Turkish: *susam*

Sesame seeds are very oily, very nutritious and have been used in Middle Eastern cuisine for a very long time.

SOYA YOGHURT

Yogurt is an integral part of Middle Eastern cuisine and served with almost every meal. In many countries it is also very popular in summer as a refreshing drink, diluted with water.

SUMAC

Sumac is a spice made from the dried and grated fruit of the staghorn sumac tree. It has a fruity, tart note and is therefore used to round off salads and rice dishes. Sumac is available in Middle Eastern and Iranian shops.

TAHINI

Also called tahina. An oily paste made of roasted sesame seeds. Tahini is used in many dishes and sauces and has a very individual and intensive flavour. The paste should be stirred well before using.

VERJUICE

This is an acidifying agent often used in Persian cuisine instead of lemon juice or vinegar.

ZA'ATAR

A mixture of ground dried herbs such as thyme, marjoram, sumac and salt. Za'atar is often augmented by sesame seeds and goes with khoubiz and salad dressings.

PERSIAN TRADITIONS WHEN PREPARING RICE

ABKESH

KATTE

This method comes from Teheran and means something like "sieved" or "washed". First, the rice is soaked for an hour in four times the quantity of salted water, then cooked briefly in lots of salty water until it is firm to the bite and then finished off in a rice cooker or a pan. In the meantime, the rice is washed and rinsed several times under running water until the water runs clear. The aim is to wash out the starch and when cooking to have separate, fluffy grains of rice.

This method is common in northern Persia, a traditional rice-growing area. As freshly harvested rice needs little liquid to ensure it is cooked through, this method requires less time. When cooking rice following the "katte" method, the rice is not washed but is merely briefly rinsed to remove any impurities, and then cooked. As a result, it contains more starch but also more nutrients, but sticks together more and the grains are less likely to be separate.

RECIPES

ABOUT THE QUANTITIES

MEZZE

Serving mezze, several small dishes, is traditional in Middle Eastern cuisine. The dishes designated as mezze are designed for two to four people depending on how many dishes are included in the mezze. Mezze dishes can, of course, also be eaten as main courses. In this case, the quantities in the ingredients' lists must be doubled or multiplied accordingly by the number of people eating the dish.

MAIN COURSES

Main courses are designed for two people, or exceptionally for more where indicated.

SIDE DISHES

Some recipes intended as side dishes can be adapted as a main course for four people.

DESSERTS

Desserts are calculated as being sufficient for six to eight people with a few exceptions.

IRAN

Soya yogurt with cucumber, rose petals and sultanas page 22
Blanched spinach with soya yogurt page 24
Aubergine mousse page 26
Citrus salad with sumac dressing, barberries and pistachios page 28
Thick pearl barley soup page 30
Broad bean stew with dill sauce page 32
Pickled gherkins, cauliflower and carrots page 34-35

MAIN COURSES

Stuffed aubergines with walnut and pomegranate page 36
Persian herb stew with beans page 38
Persian stew with split peas and crispy potato page 40
Okra in tomato sauce page 42
Persian New Year soup page 45

SIDE DISHES

Jewelled rice with barberries, almonds and pistachios page 47
Crispy saffron rice page 50
Rice with green lentils page 52
Rice with dill and broad beans page 54

INGREDIENT: Artichokes page 56

DESSERT

Persian saffron rice pudding page 58

SOYA YOGURT WITH CUCUMBER, ROSE PETALS AND SULTANAS

MAST'O KHIAR

—◇◇◇—

Preparation time: 15 minutes

1 cucumber

500 ml soya yogurt

5 sprigs of fresh mint, chopped

Salt and pepper

1 handful sultanas (approx. 25 g)

Rose petals to garnish

1 Coarsely grate the cucumber, season with salt and leave for 10 minutes. Then squeeze out well by hand and put in a bowl.

2 Mix the soya yogurt, cucumber and mint in the bowl and season to taste with salt and pepper.

3 Garnish prettily with sultanas and rose petals.

Tip: A small clove of crushed garlic can be added, according to taste.

BLANCHED SPINACH
WITH SOYA YOGURT

BORANI

Preparation time: 15 minutes

500 g spinach, well washed
    and cleaned
2 tbsp olive oil
500 ml soya yogurt
1 garlic clove, finely chopped
Salt and pepper

1 Sauté the spinach in hot oil until it wilts, then chop
coarsely and leave to cool.
2 Mix the soya yogurt, garlic and spinach together and
season well to taste with salt and pepper.

Tip: Borani can be enhanced by adding chopped raisins
and walnuts.

AUBERGINE MOUSSE

MIRZA GHASEMI

Preparation time: 45 minutes

2-3 *bulbous aubergines*
1 *large onion, finely chopped*
2 *tbsp olive oil*
3 *garlic cloves, crushed*
1 *tsp turmeric*
4 *heaped tbsp tomato purée*
125 *ml water*
Salt and pepper
2 *tbsp chopped parsley*
Juice of 1 lemon

1 Grill the aubergines preferably over an open flame. This chars the skin and gives the dish its typical taste. If this is not possible to do, prick the aubergines several times with a knife and bake in the oven at 200°C/400°F/ gas 6 until soft.

2 Halve the aubergines, carefully scrape out the flesh and chop up roughly.

3 Sauté the onion in the olive oil until golden brown, add the garlic and turmeric and fry for a further 2 minutes.

4 Add the aubergines and tomato purée to the onion mixture and continue to fry.

5 Pour in the water, season well to taste with salt and pepper and simmer on a low heat until the water has evaporated.

6 Finally, carefully add the chopped parsley and lemon juice to taste. Serve with bread as a starter, or with rice as a main course.

CITRUS SALAD WITH SUMAC DRESSING, BARBERRIES AND PISTACHIOS

——◇◇◇——

Preparation time: 10 minutes

3 oranges
1 grapefruit
2 tbsp olive oil
1 tsp sumac
Salt and pepper
3 tbsp barberries
25 g unsalted pistachio nuts
Fresh mint for sprinkling

1 Cut off the tops of the oranges and grapefruit with a knife. Now, separate the peel from the flesh in little stages using a knife. Slice gently downwards around the fruit. The fruit will then be free of its sometimes coarse peel.
2 Slice the fruits, catching the juice to be used for the marinade.
3 Mix the juice well with the olive oil and sumac and salt and pepper. Arrange the slices of orange and grapefruit on a large plate and drizzle with the marinade.
4 Sprinkle the barberries and pistachio nuts on top and serve garnished with a little fresh mint.

Tip: Coarsely chopped chicory or radicchio also go well with this salad.

THICK PEARL
BARLEY SOUP

ASHEE JOO

Preparation time: 45 minutes

1 large onion, finely chopped
1-2 tsp olive oil
½ tsp turmeric
125 g pearl barley
500 g spinach, fresh
    or frozen
1 litre vegetable stock
1½ tsp salt
150 g tinned chickpeas

1 Sweat the onion in the olive oil until transparent and add the turmeric.
2 After 2 minutes add the barley and spinach to the pan and fry for another 3 minutes.
3 Pour in the stock, season with salt and cook until the pearl barley is soft (approx. 35 min.). Then add the chickpeas and simmer for another 10 minutes.

Tip: Serve with fried onions and mint (as with *aash reshteh*, page 45-46) or lemon wedges.

BROAD BEAN STEW WITH DILL SAUCE

BAGHALI GHATOGH

Preparation time: 35 minutes

2 large onions,
    finely chopped
4 tbsp olive oil
1 bunch fresh dill
1 tsp turmeric
200 ml water
500 g frozen broad beans,
    or 250 g dried, soaked for
    2 hours in advance
2 garlic cloves, crushed
Salt
White pepper
Juice of ½ lemon

1 Sweat the onions in olive oil until transparent.

2 Chop the dill stalks very finely, chop the dill leaves coarsely and mix with the turmeric.

3 Add the dill to the onions and heat for 5 minutes, then pour in the water and season to taste with salt and pepper.

4 Add the frozen broad beans to the onion mixture (the dried beans should be soaked first in 600 ml water and then shelled). Cook covered, until the beans are soft.

5 Add the garlic and season again with salt and pepper. Simmer for 30 minutes.

6 Shortly before serving, add the lemon juice.

Tip: Serve with rice and soya yogurt.

PICKLED GHERKINS

Preparation time: 15 minutes

1 kg small pickling gherkins,
    well washed and dried
2 sprigs of tarragon
1 sprig of dill flowers
3 garlic cloves, peeled
10 peppercorns
1 tsp mustard seeds
125 ml apple cider vinegar
2 tbsp sea salt
1 sterilized jar

1   Completely fill a jar with gherkins then add the tarragon, dill flowers, garlic, peppercorns and mustard seeds.
2   Put the vinegar and salt into the jar and pour boiling water on top.
3   Seal the jar firmly and stand it upside down for 2 minutes. Store for 4 weeks before eating.

PICKLED CAULIFLOWER

Preparation time: 15 minutes

1 cauliflower, separated
    into florets (also use the
    small, light-coloured
    leaves near the stem)
1 tsp coriander seeds
3 garlic cloves, peeled
1 small, dried chilli
1-2 sprigs flowering dill
125 ml apple cider vinegar
1 tbsp salt + 1 tsp salt per jar
2 sterilized jars

1   Cut florets into bite-sized pieces and put in the sterilized jars with the cauliflower leaves. Also add the coriander seeds, garlic, chilli and dill flowers to the jars.
2   Bring 1 litre of water with 1 tablespoon salt and 125 ml cider vinegar to the boil and fill the jars whilst still boiling.
3   Sprinkle one teaspoon salt on top of each jar, seal the jars firmly and stand upside down for two minutes. Then store in a cool, dark place. Steep for at least four weeks.

PICKLED CARROTS

Preparation time: 15 minutes

400 g colourful carrots
2 garlic cloves, peeled
5 peppercorns
400 ml water
½ tbsp + 1 tsp salt
5 tbsp cider vinegar
1 sterilized jar

1 Chop up the carrots into small pieces and put into a sterilized jar with the peppercorns and garlic cloves.
2 Bring the water to the boil with ½ tbsp of salt, and the vinegar and, whilst still boiling, fill the jar.
3 Sprinkle 1 tsp salt on top, close the jar firmly and stand upside down for 2 minutes. Then store in a cool, dark place.
4 After approximately 4 weeks, the pickled carrots will be ready to eat.

STUFFED AUBERGINES WITH WALNUT AND POMEGRANATE

—◇◇◇—

Preparation time: 30 minutes
Cooking time: 1 hour

2 aubergines

2 medium-sized onions,
   chopped

1 garlic clove, crushed

A little oil

500 g ground walnuts

3 tbsp pomegranate syrup

250 ml water

Salt and pepper

100 g approx. pomegranate
   seeds

Juice of 1 lemon

A little parsley,
   for garnishing

1 Halve the aubergines, place in a generous amount of salted water and steep for half an hour.

2 Sweat the onions in a pan with some oil until transparent and add the garlic.

3 Add the walnuts and pomegranate syrup to the saucepan and slowly bring to the boil with the water.

4 Season to taste with salt and pepper and simmer on a low heat for 45 minutes, stirring regularly.

5 Add the pomegranate seeds and continue to simmer for another 15 minutes, stirring constantly.

6 Remove the aubergines from the water and wipe well with a clean cloth.

7 Cut into each aubergine flesh twice lengthways and sauté in a heated frying pan for 2-3 minutes on each side.

8 Add the lemon juice to the pomegranate and walnut mixture, and spread on the aubergines. Serve with pomegranate seeds and a little parsley as a garnish.

Tip: The nut and pomegranate filling can also be supplemented with 150-200 g strips of seitan and served with rice.

PERSIAN HERB STEW WITH BEANS

GHORME SABZI

Preparation time: 60 minutes

Serves 4

2 medium-sized onions,
    finely chopped
4 tbsp olive oil
1 tsp turmeric
Fresh, chopped herbs:
    200 g fenugreek (or 2 tbsp
        dried fenugreek),
    150 g parsley,
    100 g coriander,
    200 g spring onion or leek,
    150 g dill
1 tbsp lime powder
4 dried limes, pierced several
    times with the point
    of a knife
Salt and pepper
1 can of kidney beans
    (approx. 400 g)
Juice of 1 lemon

1   Sweat onions in oil until transparent, then add the turmeric, followed by the finely chopped herbs, and the spring onion or leek.
2   Continue to sweat, stirring constantly over a low heat until the herbs begin to take on a dark colour.
3   Add the lime powder and dried lime and cover with approx. 1 litre of water.
4   Season with salt and pepper and cook on a medium heat until the limes are very soft (approx. one hour).
5   Add the kidney beans before serving and simmer for a further 10 minutes. Finally, season to taste with lemon juice. Serve with rice.

Tip: Persian shops often stock dried mixed herbs for *ghorme sabzi*. Lime powder is made from the dried Persian lime, *limoo amani*. Both ingredients are typical of this recipe.

PERSIAN STEW WITH SPLIT PEAS AND CRISPY POTATO

KHORESHTE GHEYME

Preparation time: 30 minutes
Cooking time: 45 minutes

Serves 4

1 onion, chopped
1-2 tbsp olive oil for frying
1 tsp turmeric
1 pinch cinnamon
200 g yellow split peas,
*   washed and soaked for*
*   half an hour*
3 tbsp tomato purée
1 tin peeled tomatoes (400 g),
*   diced small*
1 knife point of saffron
3-4 dried limes, pierced
*   several times with*
*   the point of a knife*
Salt and pepper
1 pinch of sugar
300 ml water
3-4 potatoes, peeled
Sufficient oil for deep-frying
Juice of 1/2 lemon

1 Sauté the onion in the olive oil until transparent, add turmeric and cinnamon and continue to fry for 2-3 minutes until their flavour completely develops.

2 Add the split peas to the pan and stir in the tomato purée and the diced tomatoes.

3 Pound the saffron in a mortar and add it with the dried lime to the pea and tomato mixture. Season to taste with salt and pepper and a pinch of sugar.

4 Bring to the boil with 300 ml water and cook on a low heat.

5 In the meantime, cut the potatoes into thin strips and fry in oil until crispy.

6 The split peas should be cooked after about 45 minutes. Add some lemon juice, then serve in a dish with the fried potatoes arranged on top. Serve with rice.

Tip: This dish can also be served with soft-fried slices of aubergine or zucchini.

OKRA IN TOMATO SAUCE

BAMYE

—◇◇◇—

Preparation time: 30 minutes
Cooking time: 25 minutes

500 g baby okra
   (or *smallish okra pods*)
2 tbsp vinegar in 1 litre
   of water
1 onion, finely chopped
1-2 tsp olive oil
2 garlic cloves,
   finely chopped
3 tbsp tomato purée
400 g peeled tomatoes,
   coarsely chopped
250 ml vegetable stock
Salt and pepper
Juice of ½ lemon
1 tbsp fresh parsley,
   chopped

1 Shorten the okra stems and remove any brown patches without cutting into the flesh. Place in water with vinegar for 30 minutes, drain and dry well (this removes the mucilaginous substance from the okra). If using frozen okra, defrost first and then cook.

2 Sauté the onion in the olive oil until transparent, add the garlic after five minutes and fry for a further three minutes.

3 Add the okra and fry briefly.

4 Stir in the tomato purée and diced tomato and pour in the stock.

5 Season with salt and pepper and simmer gently for about twenty minutes. Shortly before serving, stir in the lemon juice and chopped parsley.

Tip: Serve with rice and soya yogurt.

PERSIAN NEW YEAR SOUP

AASH RESHTEH

Preparation time: Soak the legumes overnight
Cooking time: 2 hours

Serves 4

150 g kidney beans
150 g green or *brown lentils*
150 g chickpeas
2 litres of water
1 tbsp salt
2 large onions, finely chopped
2 garlic cloves, chopped
1½ tsp turmeric
1 kg spinach, cleaned
    and washed
50 g each of dill and parsley
25 g coriander
Salt and pepper
250 g reshteh
    (Persian noodles, available
    in Iranian shops)
2 tbsp plain flour

Although this soup takes some time to make, it is delicious and worth all the effort! This very substantial dish can be eaten as a starter but also as a nutritious meal in itself.

1 Soak the legumes overnight in water.
2 Bring 2 litres of water with 1 tablespoon of salt to the boil and cook the pulses gently.
3 Brown the onions and garlic with turmeric in a frying pan. As soon as the onions have changed colour, add to the pan of beans.
4 Coarsely chop the spinach and herbs and also add to the beans. Season to taste with salt and pepper.
5 Continue to cook until the beans are soft.
6 Add the *reshteh*, make a paste with the flour and a little cold water and stir slowly into the soup until it has a thick and creamy consistency.

Turn over →

→ *Continued*

Garnish:

1 onion, halved and sliced
1 tbsp olive oil
2 tbsp chopped garlic
3 tbsp dried mint
4 tbsp olive oil
3-5 tbsp soya yogurt

1 Slowly caramelise the onion in the olive oil and set aside.
2 Carefully fry garlic until golden brown and also set aside.
3 Sauté the mint in four tablespoons of olive oil and also set aside. Divide the soup into portions and decorate with a little soya yogurt, the fried onion, garlic and mint.

Tip: Mint also helps the digestion process. If you are unable to obtain *reshteh*, use coarsely chopped linguine noodles as an alternative.

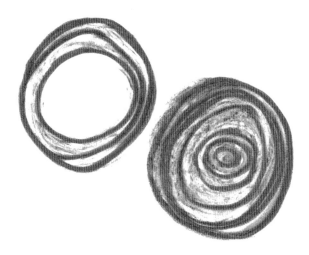

JEWELLED RICE WITH BARBERRIES, ALMONDS AND PISTACHIOS

GOHAR NESHAN POLO

—◇◇◇—

Method: *Abkesh*
Preparation time: 1 hour
Cooking time: 1 hour

450 g best basmati rice, well washed and soaked for at least 1 hour in 1 litre of salted water
2-4 tbsp vegetable oil
Salt
1 tsp saffron threads finely pounded in a mortar with 1 sugar cube

1 Bring 3 litres of water with 1 level tablespoon of salt to the boil.
2 Strain the soaked rice and put it into the boiling water.
3 Boil for a maximum of 3-4 minutes, stir occasionally and then strain (test to see if the rice is cooked; it should still have a little bite).
4 Cool the strained rice immediately under cold running water to stop it cooking.
5 Put the rice into a rice cooker or a large coated pan, add 2 tablespoons of oil and stir carefully 2-3 times.
6 Place a clean tea-towel between the pan lid and the pan, and finish cooking the rice for 45-60 minutes on a low heat.
7 Add a little more oil to the rice and stir carefully.
8 Dissolve the saffron in 50 ml hot water, and dye approximately 2 ladles of rice with it. Set it aside.

Tip: The rice should be fluffy and not sticky. It can also be served mixed with nuts and fruits.

Turn over →

→ Continued

Garnish:
1 handful each (approx. 25 g)
   sultanas and barberries
3 tbsp high quality
   margarine
Peel of 3 oranges
3 tbsp sugar
1 pinch of saffron
150 ml water
50 g almond slivers
50 g unsalted pistachio nuts,
   cut into slivers

1   Sweat the barberries and sultanas separately in a frying pan with margarine and a little sugar for 5 minutes and allow to cool.

2   Carefully remove the peel from the oranges, without any pith, and cut into strips. Simmer with the 3 tablespoons of sugar and a little ground saffron in water for 10 minutes. Strain and leave to cool.

3   Now arrange the reserved rice on a large plate and create a star shape by arranging the barberries, sultanas, almonds, pistachios, orange peel and saffron rice on top.

CRISPY SAFFRON RICE

———◇◇◇———

Method: *Katte*
Preparation time: 1 hour
Cooking time: 1 hour

300 g best basmati rice,
    well washed
3 tbsp vegetable oil
Salt
1 tsp saffron threads finely
    pounded in a mortar
    with 1 sugar cube
3-4 potatoes, peeled and cut
    into slices 1 cm thick

This famous Persian rice should be offered at every meal!

1 Put the rice with 500 ml water and a good pinch of salt and 2 tablespoons of oil into a rice cooker and bring to the boil. If you don't have a rice cooker, fry the rice in oil briefly until transparent, pour on the water and bring to the boil. Turn down the heat.

2 Stir once and then place a clean tea-towel between the pan lid and the pan. Cook until almost all the water has evaporated, but the rice is not yet quite dry.

3 Transfer the rice to another container and set aside.

4 Put enough oil (approx. 3-4 tablespoons) in the pan to cover the bottom and line with slices of potato.

5 Dissolve the saffron in about 50 ml water and add to the pan.

6 Carefully arrange the reserved rice on top of the potatoes.

7 With a cloth between the pan lid and the pan, cook until crispy on a low temperature for 30-45 minutes.

8 Add a little more oil to the rice and stir carefully.

Tip: This rice can be turned out like a sort of cake; or you can take the rice out of the pan first, break the crispy potato rice mixture into pieces and serve the two together. You can also use pieces of lavash bread instead of potatoes. Lavash is a thin, Persian white bread, similar to a Turkish dürüm wrap or a tortilla.

RICE WITH GREEN LENTILS

ADAS POLO

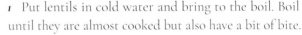

Method: *Abkesh*
Preparation time: 1 hour
Cooking time: 1 hour

100 g green lentils
300 g best basmati rice,
well washed and soaked
for at least 1 hour in
1 litre salted water
2-4 tbsp vegetable oil
Salt

1 Put lentils in cold water and bring to the boil. Boil until they are almost cooked but also have a bit of bite.
2 Bring 2 litres of water with 1 level tablespoon of salt to the boil.
3 Strain the soaked rice and put it in the boiling water with the lentils.
4 Boil for 4-5 minutes, stirring occasionally and then strain. (The rice should not be too soft, but still have a bit of bite).
5 Cool the strained rice under cold running water immediately to stop it cooking.
6 Put the rice and lentils into a rice cooker or a large coated pan, add 2 tablespoons of oil and stir carefully a few times, turning the mixture over.
7 Place a clean tea-towel between the pan lid and the pan, and finish cooking the rice for 45 minutes on a low heat.
8 Add a little more oil to the rice, turn it over carefully and fluff it up.

RICE WITH DILL AND BROAD BEANS

BAGHALI POLO

Method: *Abkesh*
Preparation time: 2 hours
Cooking time: 1 hour

300 g best basmati rice, well washed and soaked for at least 1 hour in 1 litre salted water

500 g fresh broad beans, shelled and cooked (or 200 g dried broad beans soaked in warm water for 2 hours and then cooked until al dente, then removed from their shells and sliced)

100 g dill, chopped

2-4 tbsp vegetable oil

Salt

1 Bring 2 litres of water with 1 level tablespoon of salt to the boil.

2 Strain the soaked rice and put it in the boiling water.

3 Boil for a maximum of 4-5 minutes, stirring occasionally and then strain. (The rice should not be too soft, but still have a bit of bite.)

4 Cool the strained rice immediately under cold running water so that it cannot continue cooking.

5 Mix the dill and beans together.

6 Mix the rice with the dill and beans in a rice cooker or a large, coated pan.

7 Add 2 tablespoons of oil and stir carefully.

8 Place a clean tea-towel between the pan lid and the pan, and finish cooking the rice for 45 minutes on a low heat.

9 Add a little more oil to the rice, turn it over carefully.

Tip: Frozen broad beans can also be used. Defrost the beans and then press carefully out of the shell. This rice is a classic in Persian cuisine and eaten at New Year. It is served with a little saffron rice.

ARTICHOKES

———◇◇◇———

The artichoke, a species of thistle, comes from the Middle East. *Cynara cardunculus* was known in Egypt as early as 500 B.C., but the artichoke arrived in Europe much later. It was first discovered by the Italians to be a gourmet vegetable and then by the Spanish and the French. This tender plant has been grown in Europe since the Middle Ages. The artichoke was designated Medicinal Plant of the Year in 2003.

PERSIAN SAFFRON RICE PUDDING

SHOLE ZARD

150 g rice
1 tsp saffron threads, ground
500 g sugar
100 g high-quality vegetable margarine
100 g almond flakes
100 ml rosewater
Almond flakes
Ground cinnamon

1 Bring 2 litres of water to the boil.
2 Wash the rice well and add to the boiling water.
3 Boil and stir the rice until it is quite soft and disintegrated.
4 Thoroughly dissolve the saffron in a little hot water.
5 Add the sugar and saffron solution to the rice and continue to stir until the sugar has completely dissolved.
6 Mix in the margarine and simmer for a further 5 minutes.
7 Add the almond slivers and rosewater and continue to cook for 3 minutes.
8 Continue stirring, so that nothing sticks to the bottom of the pan.
9 Pour into bowls or glasses while still hot and allow to cool.
10 Decorate with almond flakes and cinnamon.

Tip: This dessert is eaten cold.

ARMENIA

CHICKPEAS WITH SPINACH

NIVIK

Preparation time: 30 minutes

1-2 tbsp olive oil
1 large onion, chopped
1 pinch each of pepper,
    cumin and ras el hanout
2-3 tbsp tomato purée
1 tbsp agave syrup
500 g chickpeas (precooked)
750 g fresh spinach,
    washed, cleaned and
    coarsely shredded
Salt and pepper
Juice of ½ lemon

1 Heat the olive oil and slowly sweat the onion until transparent. Add spices.
2 Add tomato purée, some salt, pepper and agave syrup and mix well.
3 Mix the chickpeas with the onion mixture.
4 Sauté for 10 minutes on a medium heat, stirring frequently.
5 Mix in the spinach and simmer for 10 minutes with the lid on.
6 Season to taste with salt, pepper and lemon juice, and serve.

Tip: Serve with pickles, salad or bread as a light meal.

CHICKPEAS IN AN EARTHENWARE POT

—⬦⬦⬦—

Preparation time: 35 minutes

500 g chickpeas, rinsed
    and drained
50 ml water
2 medium-sized, floury po-
    tatoes, cooked and peeled
White pepper, ground
Salt

Filling:
3 large onions, halved
    and sliced in strips
Water
¼ tsp allspice
½ tsp cumin, whole
½ tsp black pepper, whole
2 tbsp pine nuts
2 tbsp raisins
1 tbsp tahini
Salt
A little olive oil

1 Blend the chickpeas with a little water in the blender to a fine purée.

2 Mash the potatoes with a fork. Add to the chickpeas, season with salt and white pepper and blend again.

3 Completely cover the onions with water and simmer in a covered pan for 10 minutes.

4 Remove the lid and continue to simmer. As soon as all the liquid has evaporated, put the onions in a dish and set aside.

5 Grind the allspice, cumin and black peppercorns in a mortar then mix with the onions.

6 Mix the pine nuts and raisins into the onion mixture and purée with the hand blender.

7 Fold in the tahini, season with salt and stir well.

8 Put enough chickpea mixture in an earthenware pot to cover the base. Then add a layer of onion mixture and then carefully add the remaining chickpea mixture on top and smooth it down.

9 Brush with olive oil and bake in the oven at approx. 200°C /400°F/gas 6 until golden brown.

Tip: Serve with tomato and coriander salad, and soya yoghurt.

TOMATO AND CORIANDER SALAD

Preparation time: 10 minutes

500 g colourful varieties
   of tomato
1 small garlic clove
1 handful of fresh coriander
   leaves, coarsely chopped
Juice of 1 lemon
2 tbsp olive oil
1 knife point of mace
Salt and pepper

1 Slice some of the tomatoes, and quarter the rest.
2 Chop the garlic finely and press firmly with the back of a knife so that all the essential oils can develop completely.
3 Put the tomatoes and coriander in a bowl.
4 Make a marinade by mixing together the lemon juice, garlic, olive oil and mace and pour over the tomatoes.
5 Season to taste with salt and pepper and mix well.

LENTIL SOUP

⬥⬥⬥

Preparation time: 30 minutes

1 onion, chopped
1-2 tbsp olive oil
½ tsp black caraway, whole
½ tsp coriander seeds
½ tsp cumin, whole
1 pinch of mace
1 bay leaf
1 carrot, grated
(3/4c) 150 g red or yellow lentils,
    rinsed briefly under water
1 litre water or
    vegetable stock
Salt and pepper
3 sprigs of mint,
    coarsely chopped
1 lemon, cut into in wedges

1 Sweat the onion slowly in a little olive oil until transparent.

2 Finely grind spices in mortar and sauté for 1-2 minutes with the onion.

3 Mix in the carrot and lentils.

4 Deglaze with water or vegetable stock and bring to the boil with the bay leaf.

5 Cook the soup until the lentils are soft (approx. 30 min.). Season to taste with salt and pepper.

6 As soon as the lentils are soft, remove the bay leaf and purée the soup with the hand blender until smooth. If the consistency of the soup is too thick, add a little more hot water.

7 Serve with chopped mint and lemon wedges.

DATES

———◇◇◇———

Dates are the fruit of the date tree *(phoenix dactylifera)*, a cultivated plant found originally in the Persian Gulf. It can trace its use back over several millennia. Alexander the Great is said to have relished the "bread of the desert" during his Persian campaign. In Ramadan, the fast is traditionally broken at sunset with a date and a glass of water. Dates are rich in natural sugar and also a good source of potassium, calcium, magnesium, iron and dietary fibre.

MANTE STUFFED
WITH SQUASH

Preparation time: 45 minutes

Pastry:

200 g plain flour
½ tsp salt
25 ml oil
50 ml cold water

Filling:

1 small onion, finely chopped
500 g butternut squash,
    peeled and finely sliced
3 tbsp oil
2 tbsp finely chopped parsley
Salt and black pepper
Oil for the baking tin

To finish:

150 ml vegetable stock made
    from the squash peel,
    seeds and the flesh

1 Put the flour and salt in a bowl and slowly mix with 1 tablespoon of oil. Add water and knead into a soft dough. Allow to rest for 30 minutes.

2 Sauté onion and squash in 2 tablespoons of oil until the squash is soft. Then mash gently with a fork.

3 Season to taste with parsley, salt and pepper.

4 Roll out the dough thinly and cut into squares measuring 4 x 4 cm. Fill each one with the seasoned squash mixture and press together on two sides so that the pockets are open at the top.

5 Grease the baking tin with oil and place the pastry pockets in it.

6 Bake for 20 minutes at 180°C/350°F/gas 4.

7 Boil up 150 ml vegetable stock, squash peel and seeds and pour over the pastry pockets. Bake again until all the liquid has evaporated.

Tip: Serve with soya yoghurt.

STUFFED VINE LEAVES

Preparation time: 1 hour 15 minutes

Filling:

1 large onion, finely chopped

1-2 tbsp olive oil

1 tsp allspice, crushed
   in a mortar

½ tsp turmeric

150 g rice

25 g raisins, soaked in a little
   hot water until soft

30 g pine nuts

2 tbsp finely chopped dill

Salt

Black pepper

To finish:

1 jar pickled vine leaves
   (approx. 400 g)

Water

1 lemon, finely sliced

Olive oil

1 Sauté the onion in olive oil until transparent, then add the allspice and turmeric and cook for 1-2 minutes until the flavour of the spices has developed fully.

2 Add the rice, cook for 3 minutes and add 150 ml water.

3 As soon as the liquid has been absorbed, mix the raisins, pine nuts, dill, salt and pepper into the rice, cover and put to one side.

4 Soak the pickled vine leaves in fresh water for approx. 15 minutes and strain well.

5 Place 1 large vine leaf or 2 smaller ones with the shiny side facing downwards onto a base and then cover the lower end (near the stalk) with 1 heaped tablespoon of rice. Roll it over once, then fold in the sides and then finish rolling it up. Repeat, until the stuffing has been used up.

6 Line the base of a deep saucepan or casserole with vine leaves and layer the stuffed vine leaves closely to one another in the pan.

7 Cover each layer with slices of lemon.

Turn over →

→ *Continued*

8 Lay slices of lemon on the topmost layer and cover over with vine leaves.

9 Then pour approx. 250 ml water and some olive oil over the vine leaves and weight down with a plate.

10 Bring to the boil slowly and simmer on a low heat for 30 minutes.

11 Remove from hob and allow to cool down slowly in the pan.

12 Remove the plate and carefully remove the vine leaves. Discard the lemon slices.

Tip: This dish can be eaten hot, warm or cold. Stuffed vine leaves are a classic dish in Middle Eastern cuisine, are cooked in various different ways in almost every region and are served as mezze, starter or as a main course.

CINNAMON TEA

Preparation time: 10 minutes

2 tbsp black Assam tea
500 ml water
1 cinnamon stick per glass

1 Pour hot water on the tea and allow to simmer on the lowest heat setting for 10 minutes.

2 Half-fill each cup with tea and pour hot water on top.

3 Serve with a stick of cinnamon in each tea glass.

PRESERVED LEMONS

——◇◇◇——

10 organic lemons, washed
    well under warm water
10 level tbsp sea salt
1 cinnamon stick
2 bay leaves
5 peppercorns
1 small, dried chilli
Juice of 1 lemon
Olive oil
1 large sterilised jar
    (1 litre net weight)

A wonderful way of emphasising the taste of this fruit!

1 Cut crosses into the lemons without cutting right through them.

2 Put 1 level tablespoon of sea salt into each lemon.

3 Squash as many lemons as possible into the preserving jar and leave in a cool, dark place for a week.

4 After a week, squeeze the lemons firmly to remove as much juice as possible.

5 Add the cinnamon stick, peppercorns, bay leaves and chilli to the jar and fill with freshly squeezed lemon juice, if they are not already covered by their own juice.

6 Finally, pour a good quantity of olive oil on top and close the lid again.

7 The preserved lemons should be ready to use after 4-6 weeks. The lemons will have a jelly-like consistency.

Tip: The longer the lemons are left to marinate, the better they taste.

SYRIA
LEBANON
JORDAN

◈

HUMMUS
WITH CURRY

Preparation time: 10 minutes

250 g tinned chickpeas
2 tbsp tahini
Juice of 1 lemon
3 tbsp olive oil
2-3 tsp curry powder, sweet
1 garlic clove, crushed
Salt and pepper

1   Strain the chickpeas. Purée all the ingredients in a blender.
2   Check seasoning and add more, if necessary.

Sprinkle with a little paprika and serve drizzled with olive oil. Serve with khoubiz or pitta bread.

HUMMUS WITH
CORIANDER

Preparation time: 10 minutes

250 g tinned chickpeas
2 tbsp tahini
Juice of 1 lemon
3 tbsp olive oil
½ bunch or 30 g fresh
   coriander, coarsely
   chopped
1 garlic clove, crushed
Salt and pepper

1   Strain the chickpeas. Purée all the ingredients in a blender.
2   Check seasoning and add more, if necessary.

Garnish with fresh coriander leaves and serve drizzled with olive oil. Serve with khoubiz or pitta bread.

FRIED OKRA

Preparation time: 30 minutes
Cooking time: 20 minutes

500 g okra
1 litre water + 1 tbsp vinegar
100 ml olive oil
Salt
Lemon wedges

Okra prepared in this way is also known as "Green Asparagus of the Middle East".

1   Shorten the okra stems and remove any brown patches without cutting into the flesh. Soak in 1 litre of water and vinegar for half an hour. This removes the mucilaginous substance from the okra.
2   Then remove the okra from the water and dry well.
3   Heat the oil in a deep pan, add the okra and fry on a medium heat. Turn the okra over carefully so that they brown on all sides.
4   As soon as they are slightly brown, remove and salt lightly.
5   Serve whilst still warm, with lemon wedges as a garnish. Can also be eaten as a snack.

LENTIL STEW WITH SWISS CHARD

Preparation time: 45 minutes

200 g brown lentils
600 ml water
8-10 Swiss chard leaves
1 large onion, finely chopped
1-2 tbsp olive oil
1 garlic clove, finely chopped
1 bunch or 60 g roughly
   chopped coriander
Salt
Black pepper
Juice of 1 lemon
Lemon wedges to serve

1 Rinse the lentils thoroughly and slowly bring to the boil in a pan of cold water. Simmer covered for 30 minutes (or until the lentils are cooked).
2 Clean the chard well, remove the stalk (which can be used in another dish) and halve lengthways with a knife and chop coarsely.
3 Sweat the onion in the olive oil until transparent and add the garlic, sweat for a short while longer.
4 Add the chard and sauté until it is soft.
5 Add the onion and chard mixture to the lentils.
6 Add the coriander, salt and pepper and round off with lemon juice.
7 Simmer covered on a low heat for 15 minutes.

Tip: Serve with lemon wedges and khoubiz.

HUMMUS

Preparation time: 10 minutes

250 g chickpeas in a jar
2 tbsp tahini
Juice of 1 lemon
4 tbsp olive oil
½ tsp cumin, ground
1 garlic clove, crushed
Salt and pepper
3-4 tbsp water

1   Strain the chickpeas. Purée all the ingredients in a blender.
2   Check seasoning and add more, if necessary.

Tip: Sprinkle with a little paprika powder and serve drizzled with olive oil. Serve with khoubiz or pitta bread.

TAHINI AND PARSLEY DIP

Preparation time: 5 minutes

2 garlic cloves
½ tsp coarse sea salt
75 ml tahini
50 ml water
5 tbsp lemon juice
50 g (approx.) finely
    chopped parsley

1   Crush the garlic with the salt in a mortar. Blend slowly with the tahini.
2   Mix in water and lemon juice alternately.
3   Fold in ¾ of the parsley and use the rest as a garnish.
4   Add more water or lemon juice depending on the desired consistency.

Tip: Water thickens the dip; lemon juice makes it thinner again.

TOMATO AND CUCUMBER SALAD WITH MINT

Preparation time: 5 minutes

250 g colourful types
  of tomato
2 mini cucumbers
30 g (approx.) mint
Salt and pepper
Juice of 1 lemon
Olive oil

1 Slice the tomatoes.
2 Peel the cucumbers and slice.
3 Chop the mint and mix with the tomato and cucumber.
4 Season to taste with salt, pepper, lemon juice and olive oil.

Tip: Goes well in a breakfast mezze with hummus and tahini dip.

AUBERGINE MOUSSE WITH TAHINI

BABA GHANOUSH

—◇◇◇—

Preparation time: 25 minutes

2 aubergines
2 tbsp tahini
Juice of 1-2 lemons
1 garlic clove, crushed
Salt and pepper
30 g (approx.) parsley,
    finely chopped
1 handful of pomegranate
    seeds for decorating
Olive oil

1 Grill the aubergines preferably over an open flame. This chars the skin and gives the dish its typical taste. If this is not possible to do, prick the aubergines several times with a knife and bake in the oven at 200°C /400°F/ gas 6 until soft.

2 Halve the aubergines, carefully scrape out the flesh and chop up roughly.

3 Mix the tahini, lemon juice, garlic, salt, pepper and half the parsley to make a creamy sauce. Mix with the chopped aubergine.

4 Check the seasoning and add more, if necessary.

5 Sprinkle the remaining parsley and the pomegranate seeds on top and drizzle with a little olive oil.

Tip: Warm khoubiz goes well with this dish.

LEBANESE BREAD

KHOUBIZ

Preparation time: 25 minutes

750 g plain flour
1½ tsp salt
1 sachet (25 g) fresh yeast
1 tsp sugar
300 ml warm water
2 tbsp vegetable oil

1 Put flour in a large bowl and warm on a low temperature in the oven.

2 Thoroughly mix the flour with the salt.

3 Make a hollow in the middle, crumble the yeast into it, add the sugar and pour a little lukewarm water over the yeast. Stir until the yeast and sugar have dissolved.

4 Gradually add the remaining water and knead everything together thoroughly.

5 Continue to knead until it is no longer sticky.

6 Pour the oil into a bowl, and turn the ball of dough around in it until it is completely coated in oil.

7 Cover and allow the dough to rise in a warm place until it has doubled in size (1-2 hours).

8 Knead again briefly and divide into 8 little balls.

9 Place on a cloth lightly dusted with flour and cover with another cloth. Allow to prove for 20 minutes.

10 Pre-heat the oven to 240°C/475°F/gas 9. Grease the baking sheet with a little olive oil and warm it up in the oven.

11 As soon as the oven has reached the right temperature, roll out each little ball into a flatbread, place on the sheet for 4-5 minutes and put in the oven.

12 Bake for 5 minutes. Do not open the door during baking. Then turn the bread over and bake for another 3 minutes.

13 The bread should be white and soft and have a pocket in the middle.

KHOUBIZ WITH ZA'ATAR

As described on the previous page. Brush a little oil on the flatbreads and sprinkle each one with 1 tbsp of *za'atar* before baking.

PEPPER SALAD

Preparation time: 15 minutes

3 red peppers
3 tbsp pine nuts
1 pinch of cumin
1 pinch each of paprika
    and ras el hanout
1 garlic clove, chopped
2 tbsp parsley, freshly chopped
Juice of 1 lemon
3 tbsp olive oil
Salt and pepper

1   Grill the peppers and turn them until the skins begin to bubble, then carefully remove the skins. Reserve the escaping juices and put in a bowl.
2   Cut the peppers into strips.
3   Mix with pine nuts, cumin, paprika, ras el hanout, garlic and parsley.
4   Dress the ingredients with lemon juice and olive oil and season to taste with salt and pepper.

WHITE BEAN HUMMUS

Preparation time: 15 minutes

400 g tin white beans
2 tbsp tahini
Juice of 1 lemon
1 pinch of paprika
1 pinch of ras el hanout
1 garlic clove
Salt and pepper
3-4 tbsp water

1   Strain the beans and purée all the ingredients in a blender. Season well to taste.

Tip: Serve with paprika salad.

LEBANESE BREAD SALAD

FATTOUSH

—⬦⬦—

Preparation time: 15 minutes

2 spring onions

2 mini cucumbers

250 g tomatoes

1 small, red onion

2 khoubiz or old white
   bread, torn into pieces

1 bunch of peppermint

Juice of 1 lemon

1 tbsp sumac

Salt and pepper

4 tbsp olive oil

1 Cut up the vegetables into small pieces as desired and put in a salad bowl.

2 Fry the bread in a pan in 1 tablespoon of olive oil until crisp.

3 Mix the salad ingredients with the crispy bread and the coarsely chopped mint.

4 Prepare a dressing from the lemon juice, sumac, salt, pepper and the remaining 3 tablespoons of olive oil and pour over the salad.

5 Toss well and allow to stand for 30 minutes.

SWISS CHARD

Swiss chard has been cultivated for around four thousand years and is said to have been popular with the ancient Greeks, Babylonians and ancient Egyptians.

Botanically, *beta vulgaris* is seen as a beet and is related to beetroot and sugar beet. Swiss chard has also been cultivated in Europe since the Middle Ages. For a time, chard was more popular than spinach in Europe.

STUFFED COURGETTES

—◇◇◇—

Preparation time: 45 minutes

4 round courgettes
1 onion, diced small
1-2 tbsp olive oil
½ tsp turmeric
1 pinch of cumin
1 tomato, diced
150 g rice, cooked
25 g raisins
2 tbsp chopped parsley
25 g pine nuts
Salt and pepper

1 Cut the tops off the courgettes and carefully scoop out the flesh with a spoon or a melon baller and put to one side with the tops.

2 Sauté the onion in olive oil until it starts to brown.

3 Add the spices and fry briefly.

4 Finely chop the courgette flesh, add with the tomatoes to the onions and fry for 5 minutes.

5 Put the rice, raisins, parsley and pine nuts in the pan, season with salt and pepper and mix everything together well.

6 Check the seasoning again, season if necessary and allow the mixture to cool briefly.

7 Fill the courgettes with the rice mixture and press down lightly. Close using the courgette tops and bake in the oven for 30 minutes at 180°C/350°F/gas 4.

Tip: Serve either with soya yoghurt or a tomato sauce.

POTATO KIBBEH

◇

Preparation time: 1 hour

Serves 4

*750 g potatoes, cooked
    and mashed*
*200 g bulgur, soaked for
    20 minutes in the same
    quantity of water and
    well squeezed out*
1 medium-sized onion, grated
3 tbsp chopped parsley
*1 tsp dried mint, or
    1 tbsp fresh, chopped mint*
½ tsp cinnamon
2-3 tsp salt
Black pepper
Plain flour, if necessary
*50 g chopped walnuts,
    if desired*

To finish:

*1 large onion, halved
    and sliced*
Approx. 100 ml olive oil

1 Season the mashed potato, bulgur and grated onion with parsley, mint, cinnamon and 2 teaspoons of salt and a quantity of pepper.

2 Knead the mixture thoroughly by hand. If the consistency is too soft, add flour until there is a firm mixture.

3 Layer the onion and, if desired, chopped walnuts in an oven-proof dish and pour olive oil over it until it is half covered.

4 Carefully put the potato mixture on top of the onion and smooth it down.

5 Score a diamond pattern into the potato.

6 Brush with a little olive oil and bake in the oven at 180°C /350°F/gas 4 until golden brown.

Tip: Leave to cool for 10 minutes and serve with a tomato and coriander salad, and tahini and soya yoghurt.

STUFFED SWISS
CHARD LEAVES

Preparation time: 45 minutes

Filling (serves 4):

1 bunch of spring onions,
cleaned and chopped
1-2 tbsp olive oil
150 g basmati rice
250 g brown lentils,
precooked and drained
50 g finely chopped parsley
½ tsp allspice
Salt and black pepper

To finish:

2 garlic cloves
½ tsp coarse sea salt
5 tbsp lemon juice
1 tsp dried mint
1½ kg Swiss chard, stalk
removed; leaves divided in
the middle and blanched
briefly in boiling water or
steamed in a steamer
for 3-5 min.
250 g peeled tinned tomatoes,
coarsely chopped

1 Sauté the spring onions for 2-3 minutes in olive oil and add the remaining ingredients for the filling. Briefly mix together and add 100 ml water. Simmer until the water has evaporated. Season to taste with salt and pepper.

2 Crush the garlic in a mortar with salt and mix with lemon juice and mint.

3 Place 1-2 tablespoons of filling on the chard leaves and roll up carefully.

4 Place the chard rolls next to each other in a pan and pour the garlic and mint mixture into the gaps.

5 Also put the chopped tomatoes on top of the chard rolls and pour cold water on top (the rolls should be covered with water).

6 Simmer covered on a low heat for 30 minutes.

SWEET PASTRY

BAKLAVA

Preparation time: 45 minutes

500 g grated almonds
250 g icing sugar
1 level tbsp grated
  cardamom
150 g high-quality
  margarine
5 tbsp rosewater
2 packets vegan flaky pastry
40 g chopped, unsalted
  pistachio nuts

For the syrup:
500 g sugar
250 ml water
2 tbsp lemon juice
125 ml rosewater

1 Mix the almonds, sugar, cardamom, margarine and rosewater together.
2 Line a baking sheet with baking paper and line this with flaky pastry.
3 Spread the almond mixture carefully on top of the pastry and place the second layer of flaky pastry on top.
4 Cut right angles into the pastry with a knife right through to pastry base.
5 Bake on the bottom shelf at 180°C/350°F/gas 4 for approx. 15 minutes.
6 Then place the baking sheet on the top shelf and bake for a further 10 minutes until the pastry is golden brown.
7 Take the pastry out of the oven and cool.
8 Then spoon half of the syrup over the baklava, especially in the gaps between the pastry.
9 Shortly before serving, pour the rest of the syrup over the baklava to give it a nice shine.
10 Sprinkle the chopped pistachios on top and cover the sides with the nuts, too. Serve preferably with unsweetened cinnamon tea, or coffee.

To prepare the syrup:
1 Dissolve the sugar in water and slowly bring to the boil.
2 Simmer gently for 5 minutes.
3 Stir in the lemon juice and rosewater and cool.

EGYPT

ROASTED ALMONDS

◇◇

Preparation time: 10 minutes

250 g almonds
1 tbsp olive oil
1 pinch of sugar
Salt
1 pinch of chilli
1 pinch of ras el hanout

Mix the almonds well with the other ingredients. Line a baking sheet with greaseproof paper and spread the almonds on top. Carefully roast in a preheated oven at 180°C/350°F/gas 4 for 5 minutes.

FIGS

———◇◇◇———

Figs are eaten fresh in the countries where they are grown, because they begin to ferment very quickly. Therefore, they have to be harvested before they are fully ripe so that they can be transported to other countries.

Figs that are going to be dried are always harvested when they are fully ripe. The advantage for the drying process is that at this point the water content of the fruit is considerably less. Dried figs are a popular snack in autumn and winter in most European countries.

EGYPTIAN FALAFEL

Preparation time: 30 minutes

500 g tinned broad (fava) beans, drained

3 spring onions, cut

1 large, floury potato, cooked

50 g parsley, chopped

2 tbsp coriander, chopped

3 garlic cloves

1½ tsp salt

Black pepper

1 pinch of chilli

¼ tsp baking powder

At least 2 tbsp plain flour

Sesame seeds

Oil for frying

1 Carefully shell the beans if they are unshelled.

2 Add the rest of the ingredients, put in a food processor and purée thoroughly.

3 Mix with baking powder and flour. If the dough is too sticky, add a little more flour. Season if necessary and allow to rest for 30 minutes.

4 With damp hands, shape into patties, roll in sesame seeds and fry carefully in oil until crispy.

5 Drain on kitchen paper. Serve with bread and salad.

BEANS IN TOMATO SAUCE

———◇◇◇———

Preparation time: 45 minutes

500 g flat, green
    or *yellow beans*
5 tbsp olive oil
1 medium-sized onion,
    chopped
2 garlic cloves, chopped
400 g tin peeled tomatoes,
    diced
1 tbsp tomato purée
150 ml water
1 tbsp agave syrup
Salt
Black pepper
2 tbsp fresh chopped dill
Lemon wedges to garnish

1 Wash the beans and top and tail. Cut into 5 cm pieces and put to one side.

2 Heat the oil and slowly fry onion until transparent. Add the garlic and continue to fry.

3 Add the tomatoes, tomato purée and water and season with the agave syrup, salt and pepper.

4 Simmer, covered, for 10 minutes.

5 Add the prepared beans and chopped parsley and simmer the beans, covered, until they are tender (approx. 30 minutes).

Tip: This dish can be eaten hot, warm or cold. Alternatively, serve with a side dish of diced potatoes or rice.

STUFFED TOMATOES

—◇◇◇—

Preparation time: 45 minutes

Serves 4

12 medium-sized vine
    tomatoes
1 tbsp sugar
Salt
Freshly ground black pepper
1 large onion, chopped
3 tbsp olive oil
200 g couscous, precooked
½ aubergine, coarsely diced
    and soft fried
2 tsp chopped mint
1 tsp dried cranberries,
    chopped
Water for the baking dish

1 Remove the tops from the tomatoes and put to one side. Score the tomato skins with a knife four times down their length so that they do not burst when cooking.

2 With a spoon, carefully remove the flesh and sprinkle the inside of the hollowed out tomatoes with sugar and salt.

3 Put the tomato flesh in a frying pan and cook until tender in a little salt, pepper and half a teaspoon of sugar. Press through a sieve and put to one side.

4 Sweat the onion slowly in a little oil on a low heat until transparent.

5 Pour an equal quantity of hot water over the couscous, allow to swell up for 5 minutes and then fluff up with a fork.

6 Mix the onion, diced aubergine, mint and cranberries with the couscous and tomato juice.

7 Fill the tomatoes with the couscous and aubergine mixture and press the tops of the tomatoes in down the sides.

8 Place the tomatoes in a baking dish and add a little water.

9 Bake for 30 minutes in a pre-heated oven at 180°C/ 350°F/gas 4.

Tip: Can be enjoyed as a main course or a side dish.

BAKED VEGETABLES

⸺◇◇◇⸺

Preparation time: 1 hour

Serves 4

2 courgettes

500 g waxy potatoes, peeled

2 green peppers

300 g peeled and diced
   tomatoes, or 1 tin (400 g)
   peeled diced tomatoes

2 garlic cloves, crushed

1 tbsp agave syrup

5 tbsp olive oil

2 onions, chopped

2 tbsp fresh parsley, chopped

2 tbsp fresh dill, chopped

Salt

Freshly ground black pepper

Dill and parsley for
   garnishing

Lemon wedges to garnish

1 Dice courgettes and potatoes into 1 cm-sized pieces. Clean pepper and slice.

2 Mix tomatoes with garlic and agave syrup.

3 Brush a baking dish with olive oil and put some onion in it.

4 Put the vegetable mixture and tomato mixture in the dish alternately and season now and then with herbs, salt and pepper. Repeat until it is all in the dish.

5 Pour a little oil and sprinkle herbs on top and then bake in the oven at 180°C/350°F/gas 4 until everything is cooked. Remove lid and continue to bake for 15 minutes.

6 Sprinkle with the remaining parsley and dill.

7 Serve hot with lemon halves.

Tip: You can substitute half the courgettes with aubergines. Slice the aubergines, sprinkle with salt and let them sit for 30 minutes. Rinse and dry well before using.

BLACK-EYED BEANS
WITH SWISS CHARD

———◇◇◇———

Preparation time: 30 minutes

Serves 4-6

2 onions, sliced coarsely
    into strips
4-6 tbsp olive oil
1 pinch of cumin
¼ tsp sugar
2 tins of black-eyed beans
    (400 g each) + liquid
1 litre water
1 kg Swiss chard
Salt
2 garlic cloves, optional
1-2 tsp coarse sea salt
Juice of ½ lemon
Lemon to serve

1 Sauté the onions slowly in 2-3 tablespoons of olive oil until transparent.

2 Add the cumin and sugar and sauté for another 2 minutes.

3 Put the beans into the pan with the liquid, pour the water on top and bring to the boil.

4 Clean the chard well. Cut the stalks into 1 cm pieces, add to the beans and season with salt. Simmer, covered, for another 10 minutes.

5 Chop the chard leaves finely with a knife and add to the beans. Simmer for another 15 minutes until everything is nice and tender.

6 Grind the garlic and coarse sea salt into a paste in a mortar and mix with 2-3 tablespoons of olive oil and the lemon juice.

7 Pour over the bean dish and mix together.

8 Serve the dish with fresh lemon.

Tip: If you use fresh beans, wash the beans thoroughly and bring to the boil in a pan with lots of water. Simmer for 2 minutes, then remove from the hob and leave to rest in a covered pan for 2 hours. Then heat up again slowly, simmer for 1½ hours until the beans are cooked through. A pressure cooker will speed up the cooking process.

WHITE BEAN STEW

Preparation time: 30 minutes

Serves 4-6

1 onion, chopped
2 tbsp olive oil
1 garlic clove, chopped
1 tsp cumin
1 tin (400 g) peeled tomatoes
2 tbsp tomato purée
1 bay leaf
250 ml vegetable stock
1 tbsp agave syrup
Salt and pepper
2 tins white beans
    (400 g each)
1 tbsp parsley, chopped

1 Sauté the onion quite slowly in oil until golden brown.

2 Add the garlic and cumin and fry for a further 2 minutes.

3 Add the tomatoes, tomato purée and the bay leaf, add the stock and season with the agave syrup, salt and pepper.

4 After 10 minutes, add the strained beans to the tomato sauce and simmer for another 10 minutes.

5 Check the seasoning and stir in the chopped parsley. Serve with bread and soya yoghurt.

LENTIL RISSOLES WITH FRIED TOMATOES

Preparation time: 45 minutes

150 g brown lentils, cooked

100 g potatoes, cooked
    and peeled

3 sprigs of mint, leaves only

1 small onion

1 tbsp plain flour

2 tbsp breadcrumbs

A dash of lemon juice

Salt and pepper

2 tomatoes, cut into
    2 cm-thick slices

Olive oil

1 Put the lentils, potatoes, mint and onion in a blender and purée until smooth, mix with flour and season with lemon juice, salt and pepper.

2 Then, with damp hands, shape into little rissoles. Coat in breadcrumbs.

3 Heat some olive oil in a non-stick frying pan and fry the rissoles until crispy.

4 Sprinkle salt on the tomatoes and fry on both sides until they slowly brown.

5 Serve with the rissoles.

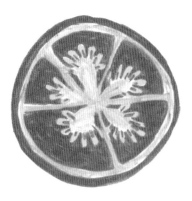

MOROCCO

TABOULEH

Preparation time: 15 minutes

75 g bulgur or couscous,
  precooked and put to cool
50 g parsley, finely chopped
50 g mint, finely chopped
3 spring onions,
  finely chopped
2 ripe tomatoes, diced
Juice of 1 lemon
Olive oil
1½ tsp salt
½ tsp black pepper

1 Put all the ingredients in a bowl.
2 Mix together the lemon juice, olive oil, salt and pepper and pour over the salad. Toss well and season again, if necessary.
3 Steep for 30 minutes.

TABOULEH WITH POMEGRANATE SEEDS AND APPLE

— ◇◇◇ —

Preparation time: 15 minutes

1-2 tart eating apples, diced
2 spring onions,
    sliced into rings
1 pomegranate, seeds
    removed from the fruit
1 tsp sumac
2 tbsp roast pine nuts
50 g mint, chopped
50 g parsley, chopped
1½ level tsp salt
½ tsp black pepper
Juice of 1 lemon
3 tbsp olive oil

1   Put all the ingredients in a bowl and season with the lemon juice and olive oil.
2   Steep for 30 minutes and then enjoy.

BAKED AUBERGINES WITH SUMAC AND PARSLEY, SERVED WITH LENTIL TABOULEH

─◇◇◇─

Preparation time: 45 minutes

2 aubergines, sliced

3 tbsp sumac

60 g freshly chopped parsley

3 tbsp olive oil for roasting

Lentil tabouleh:

1 bunch of parsley,
    finely chopped

1 bunch of mint,
    finely chopped

3 spring onions,
    sliced into fine rings

2 ripe tomatoes, diced

250 g brown lentils,
    pre-cooked and cold

1 tsp sumac

1½ tsp salt

½ tsp black pepper

Juice of 1 lemon

Olive oil

1   Add all the ingredients for lentil tabouleh to a bowl and season with lemon juice and olive oil.

2   Salt the aubergines, rub with the olive oil and bake at 180°C/350°F/gas 4 until tender.

3   Remove and sprinkle generously with sumac and parsley.

4   Serve with lentil tabouleh.

Tip: Sumac aubergines go very well with baked chicory.

CARROT BATONS WITH PRESERVED LEMONS

—◇◇◇—

Preparation time: 20 minutes

500 g carrots,
    cut into batons
1 star anise
1 cardamom pod
½ cinnamon stick
2 cloves
500 ml water
½ preserved lemon (see p. 76)
1 pinch of cumin
½ tsp salt
Pepper
Olive oil
Fresh mint for garnishing

1 Boil the carrots with star anise, cardamom, cinnamon and cloves in water until firm to the bite. Strain off water.

2 Remove pulp from the lemon and dice the peel into small pieces.

3 Mix the carrots with the lemon peel, cumin, salt and pepper and the olive oil.

4 Sprinkle a little fresh, chopped mint on top and serve while just still warm.

CARAMELISED FENNEL WITH FENNEL SEEDS AND BARBERRIES

❖

Preparation time: 20 minutes

5 tbsp olive oil
2 bulbs of fennel,
    cut lengthways in
    ½ cm-thick slices
1 tsp sugar
Salt and pepper
1 tsp fennel seeds
Zest of 1 lemon
1 tbsp barberries
1 tbsp fresh mint
Pomegranate seeds
    to garnish

1 Heat the olive oil in a frying pan.
2 Put the fennel in the hot oil, sprinkle with sugar, salt, pepper and fennel seeds and fry until golden brown.
3 Serve the fennel on a plate and grate lemon zest on top.
4 Serve garnished with barberries, pomegranate seeds and mint.

CARAMELISED BAKED VEGETABLES

———◈◈◈———

Preparation time: 25 minutes

1 kg mixed root vegetables: carrots, beetroot, parsnips, parsley roots, yellow carrots
1 tbsp coriander seeds
1 tsp cumin seeds
1 tsp fennel seeds
3 garlic cloves, whole, and squashed with the back of a knife
2 tbsp olive oil
Salt and pepper
2 tbsp agave syrup
5 sprigs of thyme and a few more to garnish
A few coriander leaves

1 Peel vegetables, clean and cut into varying sizes.
2 Grind the spices coarsely in a mortar.
3 Put the vegetables in an oven-proof dish and marinate with olive oil, the spice mixture, salt, pepper and the agave syrup. Add the sprigs of thyme.
4 Pre-heat the oven to 200°C/400°F/gas 6 and roast the vegetables for 15 minutes.
5 Garnish with coriander leaves and fresh thyme.

Tip: Serve with tahini dip, hummus or herby soya yoghurt.

ROAST HOKKAIDO WITH CORIANDER AND CHILLI OIL AND TAHINI DIP

Preparation time: 30 minutes

1 tsp cinnamon
1 tsp cumin seeds
1 tbsp coriander seeds
1 garlic clove
1 tsp coarse sea salt
1 kg hokkaido, cut into wedges
1 tbsp olive oil
1 tbsp agave syrup
Pepper

1 Grind the cinnamon, cumin, coriander seeds, garlic and sea salt in a mortar.
2 Put the pumpkin wedges in an oven-proof dish and marinate with olive oil, the spice paste and the agave syrup. Season with a little pepper.
3 Roast in a pre-heated oven at 200°C/400°F/gas 6 for 15 minutes.

TAHINI DIP

Preparation time: 5 minutes

2 garlic cloves
Salt
100 ml tahini
50-75 ml water
5-7 tbsp lemon juice

1 Crush the garlic with the salt in a mortar. Mix slowly with the tahini.
2 Stir in the water and lemon juice alternately. (**Tip:** Water thickens the dip; lemon juice makes it thinner again.)
3 Add more water or lemon juice depending on the desired consistency.

Tip: Also goes well with grilled vegetables.

CORIANDER AND CHILLI OIL

Preparation time: 5 minutes

50 g coriander seeds
1 small green chilli, halved
    and deseeded
1 garlic clove
½ tsp sea salt
6 tbsp olive oil
Zest of ½ lemon

1   Grind the coriander, chilli, garlic and sea salt in a
mortar to make a fine pulp.
2   Mix with olive oil and grate in lemon zest.
3   Spoon over the pumpkin wedges.

SAFFRON COUSCOUS WITH CARAMELISED ONIONS

Preparation time: Up to 60 minutes

300 g couscous

1 tsp salt

½ tsp saffron threads,
    well ground with a sugar
    cube in a mortar to
    create a powder

500 g onions,
    sliced into rings

25 g raisins

½ pomegranate,
    only the seeds

Mint to garnish

Olive oil

1 Mix the couscous with salt, 1 tablespoon of olive oil and the saffron and sugar mixture and pour over 350 ml hot water.

2 With a lid on, allow to swell up for 5-10 minutes and then fluff up with a fork.

3 Caramelise the onions slowly in 4-5 tablespoons of olive oil (can take up to an hour).

4 Serve the couscous on a plate, arrange the caramelised onions on top and garnish with raisins, pomegranate and mint.

Tip: If you are in a hurry, the onions can be caramelised on a higher heat. To achieve this, add a little sugar.

ORANGE AND CORIANDER RELISH

Preparation time: 15 minutes

1 red onion,
   sliced into thin rings
1 orange
Juice of 1 orange
Juice of 1 lime
1 garlic clove, chopped
40 g fresh coriander,
   chopped
Salt and pepper
A few pomegranate seeds
   for garnishing

1 Pour hot water over the onion rings and leave to stand for at least 10 minutes.
2 In the meantime, remove the orange peel with a sharp knife so that there is only the flesh left. Slice the orange.
3 Strain the onion rings and put in a bowl with the slices of orange.
4 Pour the orange and lime juice on top.
5 Season to taste with garlic, coriander, salt and pepper.
6 Serve sprinkled with pomegranate seeds.

Tip: If you prefer it a little more piquant, deseed half a chilli, chop into small pieces and add.

CORIANDER AND DATE COUSCOUS

Preparation time: 15 minutes

350 g couscous

1 tbsp olive oil

Zest of 1 organic lemon

1 tsp salt

350 ml hot water

10 dates, sliced into fine strips

30 g fresh coriander,
    finely chopped

1 Put the couscous in a bowl with olive oil, lemon zest and salt and mix using your hands.

2 Pour on boiling water.

3 Cover and leave to swell for 5 minutes.

4 Fluff up with a fork.

5 Stir in the dates and coriander.

BUTTERNUT SQUASH TAGINE WITH CORIANDER AND DATE COUSCOUS

◇◇◇

Preparation time: 35 minutes

1 medium-sized butternut squash, peeled and cut into slices 2 cm thick

2 tbsp olive oil

1 large onion, finely chopped

2 garlic cloves, finely chopped

2 tsp fresh grated ginger

1 knife point of saffron

2 tbsp coriander seeds, crushed

3 tsp cumin seeds, ground

2 tsp paprika

1 tin (400 g) diced tomatoes

250 ml passata

1 cinnamon stick

1 tsp agave syrup

500 ml water

½ bunch fresh coriander, chopped

Salt and pepper

50 g roast almond slivers to garnish

1 Heat the oil in a pan and sweat the onion until soft.

2 Add the garlic, ginger, saffron, 1 teaspoon of salt, coriander seeds, cumin seeds and paprika and fry with the onion for 2 minutes until the aroma of the spices develops fully and it is fragrant.

3 Add the tomatoes, pumpkin, cinnamon stick, agave syrup and water, season with salt and pepper and cook everything for approx. 30 minutes.

4 If necessary, add water.

5 Stir in the coriander and season to taste again with salt and pepper.

6 Prepare the coriander and date couscous, place on a plate, garnish with almond slivers and serve with cucumber and mint in soya yoghurt.

ROAST CAULIFLOWER
WITH TAHINI DIP

—◇◇◇—

Preparation time: 20 minutes

1 cauliflower, washed
   and dried
1 lemon, halved and sliced
15 olives, preferably
   Taggiasca
1 red onion, cut into wedges
2 garlic cloves, halved
Salt and pepper
1 pinch of chilli
2 tbsp pine nuts

1   Divide the cauliflower into florets and mix with the remaining ingredients.
2   Roast in a pre-heated oven at 200°C/400°F/gas 6 for 15 minutes.
3   Then sprinkle a little chilli powder and some pine nuts on top and serve with tahini dip (see p. 140).

VEGETABLE TAGINE
WITH QUINCE

Preparation time: 30 minutes

1 onion, chopped

2-3 tbsp olive oil

1 pinch of cinnamon

1 pinch of cumin

1 courgette, sliced

250 ml passata

1 quince, cut into wedges

Juice of ½ lemon

1 Sweat the onion in the olive oil until transparent.

2 Add the spices and continue to fry for 2 minutes.

3 Add the courgettes and fry briefly.

4 Add the passata and briefly bring to the boil.

5 After 15 minutes, add the quince and simmer for another 10 minutes. Season to taste with lemon juice and serve with white rice.

BRAISED FENNEL
WITH SAFFRON

Preparation time: 30 minutes

4 fennel bulbs, cut into
    quarters lengthways,
    fennel leaves put aside
    for decorating

5 shallots, peeled and halved

2 tbsp olive oil

8-10 saffron threads

10 Taggiasca olives
    or alternatively
    Kalamata olives

Salt and pepper

3 garlic cloves, in their skins

2 tbsp verjuice

1 tbsp agave syrup

250 ml vegetable stock

10 cherry tomatoes,
    quartered

Zest of 1 organic lemon

1 Sauté the fennel in oil until golden brown. Add shallots and continue to fry briefly.

2 Finely grind saffron in a mortar and add to the fennel.

3 Cook the olives with fennel and shallots and season with salt and pepper.

4 Add verjuice and agave syrup and reduce the heat.

5 Deglaze with the stock and simmer for 15 minutes.

6 Cook the cherry tomatoes with the other ingredients in the pan for the final 5 minutes.

7 Grate the lemon zest on top and serve decorated with the fennel leaves.

Tip: Serve with bread or boiled potatoes.

PEPPERS STUFFED
WITH COUSCOUS

—◇◇◇—

Preparation time: 25 minutes

1 onion, finely chopped

2-3 tbsp olive oil

1 garlic clove, crushed

1 tbsp tomato purée

350 ml vegetable stock

10 cherry tomatoes, halved

3 peppers, halved
    lengthways, and cores
    removed

200 g couscous

40 g parsley, finely chopped

Salt and pepper

1 Sauté the onion in a little oil until transparent and fry the garlic briefly as well.

2 Add the tomato purée to the pan and pour on 100 ml vegetable stock.

3 Put the couscous in a bowl and mix in ½ teaspoon of salt.

4 Pour 250 ml hot vegetable stock over the couscous, cover, and allow to swell for 5 minutes.

5 Fluff up with a fork and mix with the cherry tomatoes.

6 Place the halved peppers in an oven-proof dish, add a little salt and stuff the peppers with the couscous. Season with a little pepper.

7 Pour the remaining vegetable stock into the dish and bake for approx. 20 minutes at 180°C/350°F/gas 4 in a pre-heated oven, or until the peppers are soft, but still maintain their shape.

8 Serve with soya yoghurt.

ALMOND AND ROSE CAKE

Preparation time: 45 minutes

250 g grated almonds

250 g sugar

250 g vegan butter, or
alternatively margarine,
at room temperature

1 tbsp rosewater

1 packet of filo pastry

Rose petals to garnish

A little melted vegan butter
to brush the pastry

1 Knead the almonds, sugar, vegan butter and rosewater either in a food processor or by hand into a homogenous mass.

2 Take 3 sheets of filo pastry and lay them so that they overlap and there is a long pastry line.

3 Now spread the almond mixture on the pastry leaving 5 cm clear at the bottom edge. Then carefully roll up the pastry into a long sausage.

4 Coil this roll carefully into a greased baking tin and brush the melted butter on it.

5 Bake in the oven at 180°C/350°F/gas 4 for 20 minutes or until the pastry has turned golden brown.

6 Sprinkle with rose petals and serve preferably while still a little warm.

Tip: If you have time, you can make the filo pastry yourself. To do this, knead 500 g flour, 2 tbsp olive oil, 250 ml water, 1 tsp lemon juice and 1 pinch of salt into a dough. Leave to rest under a cloth for approximately 30 minutes. Roll out very thinly as required.

TURKEY

—◇◇◇—

HAZELNUT DIP

Preparation time: 10 minutes

100 g hazelnuts
30 g soft white breadcrumbs
2 garlic cloves, crushed
1-2 tbsp water
5 tbsp olive oil
1 tsp salt
Pepper
1 tbsp light vinegar

1 Soak the hazelnuts in hot water for 5 minutes, strain and remove skins.
2 Finely chop the hazelnuts in a blender or food processor.
3 Add the breadcrumbs, garlic and water. Slowly add the oil. Season with salt, pepper and vinegar.
4 Refrigerate for an hour.

Tip: The dip also works very well with grated almonds.

SOYA YOGHURT DIP

Preparation time: 5 minutes

1-2 garlic cloves
½ tsp coarse sea salt
250 ml soya yoghurt

1 Grind the garlic with salt in a mortar.
2 Mix with soya yoghurt.

BRAISED LEEKS WITH SAFFRON

— ◊◊◊ —

Preparation time: 35 minutes

6 medium-sized or
   3 large leeks
1 onion, sliced
3-4 tbsp olive oil
2 tbsp tomato purée
¼ tsp ras el hanout
1 knife point of saffron
1 tsp agave syrup
Salt
Black pepper, ground
1 lemon, sliced
2 tbsp lemon juice
A few sprigs of thyme
   to cook, and garnish
2 slices organic lemon
   for garnishing

1 Remove the outer leaves of the leek and clean and wash well.(**Tip:** the discarded leaves can be used to make soup).

2 Sauté the onion slowly in the olive oil, in a large pan, until soft.

3 Mix the tomato purée with 100 ml water and pour over the onion.

4 Season with ras el hanout, saffron, agave syrup, salt and pepper.

5 Slowly bring everything to the boil and allow to simmer on a low heat for 5 minutes. Stir regularly, so that nothing sticks to the bottom of the pan.

6 Place the leek and lemon slices in the sauce, pour the lemon juice on top and add a few sprigs of thyme. Add a little more water if necessary.

7 Simmer, covered, for 15 minutes (the leek should always be covered by liquid).

8 The leek should be cooked after approximately 15 minutes.

9 Serve with the remaining herbs and fresh lemon.

Tip: Serve with boiled potatoes or rice.

BÖREK STUFFED WITH SWISS CHARD

Preparation time: 20 minutes

1 onion, finely diced
3 tbsp olive oil
1 garlic clove, chopped
1.2 kg Swiss chard,
    finely chop stalk and
    coarsely chop leaves
Salt and pepper
1 packet of filo pastry

1 Sauté the onion in the olive oil until transparent then add the garlic.

2 Fry the Swiss chard as well until everything is tender.

3 Season well with salt and pepper.

4 Cut 2 square sheets of filo pastry and place the chard mixture on top. Fold the corners into the middle to form a little square. Place the lower left corner on the upper right corner. Then fold the resulting triangle in the middle to form a smaller triangle.

5 Brush the börek with olive oil and bake in the oven at 180°C/350°F/gas 4.

BRAISED ARTICHOKES

❖

Preparation time: 20 minutes

12 artichoke hearts
Juice of 2 lemons
1 lemon, quartered
1½ litres water
4 spring onions, chopped
3 carrots, peeled and cut
    into slices 1 cm thick
250 g shallots, peeled
500 g waxy potatoes, peeled
Juice of 1 lemon
5 tbsp olive oil
Approx. 300 ml water or
    vegetable stock
Salt
Black pepper
1-2 tbsp fresh dill
    or parsley, chopped
3 tsp cornflour

1 Prepare artichoke hearts. To do this, mix the lemon juice, lemon wedges and water in a large bowl. Break off the artichoke stems and remove all outer leaves until just the hearts remain. Remove the fibrous choke and clean each artichoke individually with a vegetable knife. Then put them in the bowl containing the lemon and water so that they do not discolour.

2 Put the spring onions, then the carrots and shallots, potatoes and artichoke hearts in a large frying pan.

3 Pour lemon juice and olive oil on top and then enough water or vegetable stock to just cover everything.

4 Season with salt and pepper and sprinkle fresh dill or parsley on top.

5 Simmer covered on a low heat until the vegetables are cooked.

6 Remove the vegetables from the liquid and arrange on a deep plate.

7 Mix the cornflour with a little cold water and carefully add to the liquid. Allow to simmer gently for 2 minutes until the liquid thickens. Then pour the sauce over the vegetables and garnish with herbs.

BÖREK STUFFED
WITH SQUASH

◈

Preparation time: 20 minutes

1 onion, finely chopped
3 tbsp olive oil
1 garlic clove
1 pinch of cinnamon
1 pinch of cumin
500 g butternut squash,
   peeled and grated
A dash of lemon juice
Salt and pepper
2 tbsp fresh parsley, chopped
1 packet of filo pastry

1 Sauté the onion in the olive oil until transparent, then add the garlic and spices.
2 After 5 minutes, add the squash and sauté on a low heat until the squash is completely tender. Allow to cool.
3 Season with the lemon juice, salt and pepper and stir in the chopped parsley.
4 Place filo pastry sheets and the squash filling in alternate layers in an oven-proof dish and brush with oil. Bake in the oven at 180°C/350°F/gas 4 for about 20 minutes until golden brown.

Tip: Serve with soya yoghurt.

VEGETABLE STEW
WITH WHITE BEANS

Preparation time: 30 minutes

Serves 4

2 large onions, chopped
2 tbsp olive oil
2 garlic cloves, chopped
2 carrots, sliced
2 sticks of celery, sliced
3 tbsp tomato purée
500 g tinned white beans,
    drained
1 tsp agave syrup
1 pinch hot chilli
600 ml water or
    vegetable stock
Salt and pepper
Juice of 1 lemon
1 tbsp fresh parsley, chopped

1 Sauté the onion in the oil until transparent, then add the garlic, carrots and celery and fry for another 5 minutes.

2 Add the tomato purée and beans and fry for 1 minute

3 Add the agave syrup and chilli and pour on water or stock. Cook for 10-15 minutes.

4 Season to taste with salt and pepper and add lemon juice and parsley to taste.

STUFFED AUBERGINE

IMAM BAYILDI

Preparation time: 30 minutes

Serves 4

4 bulbous or 8 long,
  slim aubergines,
  stems removed
1 litre water with 2 tbsp salt
3 medium-sized onions
5 tbsp olive oil
3 garlic cloves, cut
3 medium-sized tomatoes,
  diced
1 pinch of sugar
125 ml water
1 bunch (60 g) fresh parsley,
  chopped
2 tbsp lemon juice
Salt and pepper
2-3 tbsp olive oil for frying

1 Halve aubergines lengthways and carefully score twice from top to bottom.

2 Soak aubergine halves in plenty of salty water for 30 minutes.

3 Drain well and dry.

4 In the meantime, cut the onions in half lengthways and slice into strips.

5 Sauté in oil until soft (**Tip:** the slower the onions are cooked, the better their unique sweet flavour will develop.)

6 Add the garlic and fry for 1 minute.

7 Add the diced tomato, sugar and 125 ml water, mix in the parsley, and season well with the lemon juice, salt and pepper.

8 Sear the aubergines well in a frying pan so that they become tender but retain a bit of bite.

9 With the skin facing down, put in the dish and squeeze as much of the filling as possible into the gaps. Put the rest of the filling on top.

10 Then simmer on a low heat for 30-40 minutes or bake in the oven at 180°C/350°F/gas 4. If necessary, add more water.

Tip: Serve with pitta bread and soya yoghurt.

BAKED CAULIFLOWER WITH SOYA YOGHURT AND HAZELNUT DIP

—◇◇◇—

Preparation time: 30 minutes

1 cauliflower, cut into florets
 or slices
2 garlic cloves, chopped
2 tbsp lemon juice
3 tbsp olive oil
Salt and pepper
1 good handful
 of breadcrumbs

1 Mix the cauliflower with garlic, lemon juice, olive oil, salt and pepper.

2 Line a baking pan with greaseproof paper and place the cauliflower on top (ideally there is sufficient space between the florets to allow them to cook properly).

3 Pre-heat the oven to 200°C/400°F/gas 6 and bake the cauliflower until it is lightly browned (approx. 10 minutes).

4 Scatter breadcrumbs over the florets and turn over carefully.

5 Turn the oven down to 180°C/350°F/gas 4 and continue to bake the cauliflower for 5 minutes until the breadcrumbs have turned golden brown.

Tip: Serve with dips (i.e. hazelnut dip, soya yoghurt dip) or a salad.

TEA AND COFFEE

—◇◇◇—

In his journal about his travels to Jerusalem and the Middle East in 1573, a doctor from Augsburg described coffee as a medicine and remedy, drunk from little china bowls. The finely ground coffee was boiled several times in a long-handled pot called a *cezve* or *ibrik* and was drunk unfiltered. Turkish coffee is drunk with rosewater, whereas Arabic coffee is seasoned with cardamom or cloves.

Tea found its way to Turkey via the Silk Road. A tea culture, similar to that of the rest of the Orient, established itself from the 19th century. Strong black tea is traditionally prepared in a samovar and served in elegant tea glasses. Tea and coffee always provide an opportunity to sit down with friends and talk.

TURKISH OR ARABIC COFFEE

Preparation time: 5 minutes

*2 tsp finely ground coffee
    for approx. 180 ml water
    (for 2 people)*
2 tsp sugar
1 pinch ground cardamom

1 Mix the coffee with sugar and cardamom and pour plenty of water into a Turkish coffee pot. (**Tip:** use 2 tablespoons of coffee powder per coffee cup.)

2 Heat the coffee quite slowly and then bring to the boil.

3 It is said that the coffee must boil three times. The foam that forms in a ring on top must not close, otherwise the coffee is overboiled.

4 As soon as the coffee has been boiled three times, leave it to rest for half a minute so that as many grounds can settle as possible.

5 Then pour the coffee, with the foam, into coffee glasses.

Tip: Serve with baklava.

FIGS IN SYRUP

◇

Preparation time: 30 minutes

Serves 2

4-6 large, ripe figs
1 whole almond soaked
    and peeled, per fig
5 tbsp sugar
Grated zest of ½ lemon
Juice of 1 lemon
4 tbsp agave syrup
1 tsp dried rose petals with
    almond slivers to garnish

1   Cut a cross into each fig and stuff with an almond.
2   Dissolve the sugar with 4 tablespoons of water in a pan, stirring continuously. Add the lemon zest, lemon juice and agave syrup and mix well until there is a nice syrup.
3   Place the figs in the syrup and gently simmer for 10 minutes.
4   Spoon the syrup over the figs from time to time.
5   Serve the figs in the syrup on a plate and garnish with almond slivers and rose petals.

Tip: Serve with soya yoghurt or soya cream, or with chopped pistachio nuts.

TURKISH SEMOLINA CAKE

REVANI

Preparation time: 20 minutes
Cooking time: 35 minutes

1 pot (250 g) soya yoghurt
1 pot sugar
1 pot spelt flour, fine
1 pot hard wheat semolina,
    finely ground
½ pot sunflower oil
½ sachet cream of tartar
½ sachet vanilla sugar
2 tbsp sparkling mineral
    water
1 tbsp grated lemon peel
Pistachios, coarsely chopped

For the syrup:
250 g sugar
150 ml water
1 tsp lemon juice

1 Put the yoghurt in a mixing bowl, wash and dry the pot and use it to measure out the remaining ingredients.
2 Sieve the flour and semolina, and mix to a dough with the soya yoghurt and the remaining ingredients.
3 Line a deep 24 x 24 cm baking tin and put the dough on top.
4 Bake on the middle shelf in a pre-heated oven at 200°C/400°F/gas 6 for about 30 to 35 minutes.
5 To make the syrup, bring all the ingredients to the boil and simmer on a medium heat for 15 minutes. Let it cool until it is thick and pour on the cooled cake.
6 Decorate with pistachio nuts.

MIDDLE EASTERN
RICE PUDDING

Preparation time: 30 minutes

200 g pudding rice
1 litre almond milk,
    unsweetened
30 g whole cane sugar
1 cardamom pod
1 star anise
2 cloves
1 cinnamon stick
Pulp of 1 vanilla pod,
    halved

1 Put the milk, rice, sugar, vanilla and spices in a pan and slowly bring to the boil.
2 Stir continuously so that the rice does not stick to the bottom of the pan. The stirring helps the rice to release starch and produces a creamy consistency.
3 After about 30 minutes, the rice will be cooked and can be put into small dishes.

Tip: Instead of sugar, you can put four dried Medjoul dates into the milk, purée to a smooth consistency with a hand-held mixer or blender and continue to cook as instructed above.

ACKNOWLEDGEMENTS

I would like to thank my mother, who is the undisputed queen of Persian cuisine in our family. She passed on to me her understanding of hospitality, the love of cooking and a delight in getting small details right. Her sense of the smells and fragrances of Middle Eastern cuisine has influenced me and has been with me throughout my entire life.

I would like to thank my family, above all, my husband, who over the years has supported and spurred me on to build a career out of my passion for cooking.

And my dear Anna, without you and your sense of humour, your great mental support and our friendship, I would be lacking a great deal in my life. I extend my thanks to Arnold Pöschl for the visual interpretation of my work. You are a wonderful colleague and have become a good friend.

Enormous thanks go to Sebastian Rahs, a truly unique individual. I am so happy to have had you by my side during the project. Your creativity and great love for detail are second to none. I also thank Thomas Weber for always giving me the right input and incentives at the right moment to follow new paths and to try out new things.

Enormous thanks are due to Karin and Zahra for your hospitality and your great love of creative freedom. With your extreme generosity, putting your wonderful konoba at our disposal, enriched our work greatly. www. stancijamani.com. Many thanks, too, to Henriette Artz whose gorgeous and colourful illustrations enhance my book and reflect the colourful life of the Middle East so beautifully. Huge thanks go to Jannis Schulze for your graphics and layout. Finally, I would like to thank NeunZehn Verlag for giving me the creative space to put my wishes and ideas into practice.

MY PARTNERS:

Many thanks to Reiss, the traditional Austrian company, for your wonderful support for my project and the lovely aroma pots. Your enamel cookware is ecological, resource-friendly and focuses on sustainability and environmental compatibility at all stages of production. This is why your products perfectly suit my philosophy of consciously pursuing excellent nutrition and a sustainable lifestyle. www.riess.at

Many thanks, too, to Sonnentor whose spices I value for their high quality. Your fairly traded products fulfil the highest ecological standards and enhance all my recipes. www.sonnentor.at

My grateful thanks are extended to Sandra Haischberger at Feine Dinge for your unique and wonderful china. I wish all chefs could arrange and serve their creations on such fine crockery. www.feinedinge.at

ABOUT THE CHEF

We should enjoy our food! But perhaps enjoyment is not always uppermost in our minds when thinking about vegan food. Even if something is home-cooked, ready-made ingredients of questionable origin can often appear on the table in vegan households. In everyday life, many people feel obliged to come to terms with the manipulations of the commercial food industry. And this is what makes Parvin Razavi's cookbook so special. It can be seen as a clear statement against industrially-made ingredients, as a commitment to enjoy food and as an encouragement to renounce food products but rather to work with food. At the heart of this is the joy of trying things out, making changes and new combinations. Her Mediterranean and Persian influences are the cultural starting point for culinary explorations in lots of different directions. Legumes of all kinds are the most common ingredients, and in addition to spices such as cumin, turmeric, saffron, cinnamon, mace, ras el hanout and tahini, there are also herbs, primarily fresh coriander, mint, dill and parsley. And, not to be forgotten in Middle Eastern cuisine: (vegan) yoghurt.

But as Parvin does not only favour organic food, but also puts emphasis on seasonal and regional food, her recipes can also be taken as an invitation to experiment. Anyone who has been Parvin's guest knows that hummus is traditionally prepared with puréed chickpeas, but is equally tasty made with runner beans or based on pinto beans, broad beans or green beans.

Perhaps one can only approach the art of cooking so unreservedly if one has not 'learned' it. It is no secret that Parvin is not a trained chef; she is not a professional in the traditional sense of the word. All her skill is self taught, wrested from the routine of being a mother of two who discovered her passion was cooking. This is why her recipes are simple and easy to cook. Food should provide energy and satisfy but not leave you feeling overfull.

Her recipe collection is not to be followed slavishly. You do not need a cookbook for that approach; Google or a recipe app would fit the bill in that case. Rather, her recipes should inspire you and invite you to emulate them - while browsing, trying them out and thinking about how to conjure up a wholesome meal from the left-over vegetables sitting in the refrigerator and finally, when actually cooking.

Thomas Weber
Editor of *Biorama*,
the magazine for a sustainable lifestyle

INDEX

Published in 2017 by

Grub Street

4 Rainham Close

London, SW11 6SS

Reprinted 2018, 2019

Email: food@grubstreet.co.uk

Web: www.grubstreet.co.uk

Twitter: @grub_street

Facebook: Grub Street Publishing

Copyright © Neun Zehn Verlag 2015

Published originally in German as *Vegan Oriental*

Recipes: Parvin Razavi

Cover and book design: Daniele Roa

Food styling: Sebastian Rahs

Illustration: © Henriette Artz

Photography: © Arnold Pöschl

A CIP catalogue record for this book is available from
the British Library.

ISBN 978-1-910690-37-6

Printed and bound in the Czech Republic